Classical Themes

Favorite orchestral works arranged for piano solo
by Fred Kern, Phillip Keveren, and Mona Rejino

Text Author
Barbara Kreader

Editor
Margaret Otwell

Classical Themes Level 4 is designed for use with the fourth book of any piano method.

Concepts in *Classical Themes Level 4*:

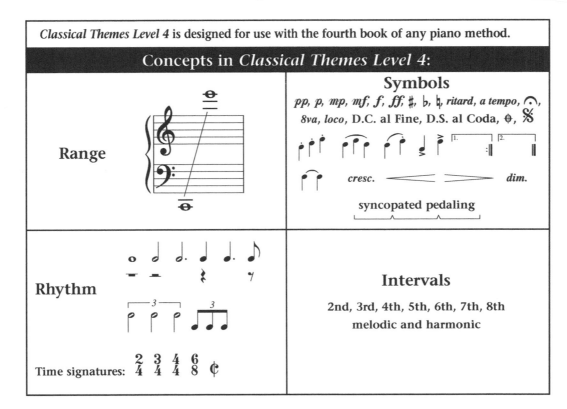

Range

Symbols

pp, p, mp, mf, f, ff, ♯, ♭, ♮, *ritard, a tempo,* 𝄐,
8va, loco, D.C. al Fine, D.S. al Coda, ⊕, 𝄋

cresc.　　　　　　　　　　　　dim.

syncopated pedaling

Rhythm

Time signatures: 2/4　3/4　4/4　6/8　¢

Intervals

2nd, 3rd, 4th, 5th, 6th, 7th, 8th
melodic and harmonic

To access audio visit:
www.halleonard.com/mylibrary

2190-3357-8500-2875

ISBN 978-1-4950-4763-3

**HAL•LEONARD®
CORPORATION**

7777 W. BLUEMOUND RD. P.O. BOX 13819 MILWAUKEE, WI 53213

In Australia Contact:
Hal Leonard Australia Pty. Ltd.
4 Lentara Court
Cheltenham, Victoria, 3192 Australia
Email: ausadmin@halleonard.com.au

Visit Hal Leonard Online at
www.halleonard.com

Table of Contents

About the Compositions

Ludwig van Beethoven (1770-1827)

The German composer Ludwig van Beethoven wrote his seventh symphony between 1811-1812, years when he knew with certainty that he was going deaf. His first symphonies, including the sixth, bear the tortured mood of a hero in a drama, fighting overwhelming odds that will eventually defeat him. With the seventh symphony, the musical focus shifts to one of acceptance, and even triumph, over tragedy. Beethoven's effortless control over the *Seventh Symphony*'s splendid orchestration and magnificent thematic integration show him at the height of his power. Beethoven lived a chaotic and difficult life. An extremely untidy man, he is known to have used first drafts of his compositions to cover the soup and even the chamber pot. Yet his personal misfortunes, chronic illnesses, and frequent quarrels with relatives and friends had no influence on his music or his ability to compose. Nicolas Slonimsky wrote, *"Beethoven ardently called for peace among men, but he could never achieve peace within himself..."*

Pyotr Il'yich Tchaikovsky (1840-1893)

During the early 1880's, the Russian composer Pyotr Il'yich Tchaikovsky penned *The Festival Overture* and *1812 Overture,* music of great beauty that is also famous for its noise and bombast. The *1812 Overture* features a cannon volley in its orchestration, a religious melody as its opening theme, and the national anthems of Russia and France. Its festive noisiness and bursts of energy make it popular even today. In the United States, orchestras frequently perform it to celebrate the Fourth of July.

Pyotr Il'yich Tchaikovsky (1840-1893)

The Russian composer Pyotr Il'yich Tchaikovsky intended his *Sixth Symphony* as the grand conclusion to his career, and he dedicated it to the Tsar. Composed between February and March of 1893, much of the work's music sounds sad and gloomy and aptly matches its nickname *"Pathetique."* Only the second movement and scherzo sound triumphant and exultant. Tchaikovsky conducted the first performance of the *Sixth Symphony* on October 16, 1893. Just five days later, he fell ill and died.

Georges Bizet (1838-1875)

When French composer Georges Bizet introduced his opera, *Carmen,* in 1875, no one could have predicted that it would become one of the great operatic masterpieces of the 19th century, with its tunes familiar to millions. No one wanted to produce *Carmen*. Its anti-heroine, the brazen Carmen, lived a life at odds with conventional family entertainment. Directors thought the plot, with its tragic ending, improper; orchestras found the music too difficult; the chorus had trouble acting as individuals rather than a group, and the women objected to having to smoke and fight onstage. Yet this *opera comique* (opera with spoken dialogue) ran for forty-five performances in 1875, with three more in 1876, and continues as one of today's most popular theatrical entertainments. Perhaps because of the strain of mounting the production, the 36-year old Bizet died of a heart attack on the night of the opera's 33rd performance.

Franz Schubert (1797-1828)

During his short lifetime, the Viennese composer Franz Schubert wrote 600 songs! When only 18, he wrote 150 songs, more than one every three days, and these included *Gretchen am Spinnrade* and *Die Erlkonig,* two of his masterpieces. Schubert's life-long love of poetry inspired him to use the words of 150 different poets in his works. He especially favored Schiller, Goethe, Heine, and Ruckert. Schubert composed his famous *Ave Maria* in the summer of 1825 during a break in the long illness that eventually caused his early death. He toured that year with the leading baritone of the day, J.M. Vogl, who frequently sang this hymn of praise to the Virgin Mary. Schubert's songs integrate words, music, and accompaniment in a strikingly new way. He wrote to his brother Ferdinand: *"The manner in which Vogl sings and the way I accompany, as though we were one at such a moment, is something new and quite unheard of ..."*

Rondeau
Jean-Joseph Mouret (1682-1738)

The PBS show "Masterpiece Theatre" uses the French composer Jean-Joseph Mouret's *Rondeau* as its theme music. Moreau's other music is rarely heard. Although he is considered the most important French composer between Lully and Rameau, his elegant and charming music sounds light-weight when heard today. Mouret served as *superintendant de musique* for the Sceaux court, Conductor of the Paris Opera, and artistic director of the prestigiou*s Concerts Spirituels.* Yet, he eventually lost all of these jobs and died penniless in an asylum.

O mio babbino caro from the opera GIANNI SCHICCHI
Giacomo Puccini (1858-1924)

The Italian composer Giacomo Puccini composed some of the world's most loved operas, such as *Madama Butterfly* and *La Bohéme.* The comedic opera *Gianni Schicchi* is the third in Puccini's trilogy of one-act operas that includes the violent *Il Tabarro* and the lovely *Suor Angelica. Gianni Schicchi's* story retells the macabre yet amusing escapades of an actual 13th-century family's fight to regain the fortune a relative has left to the town monastery. They call upon Gianni Schicchi, whose daughter, Lauretta, plans to marry into the family. In this aria, *O mio babbino caro* (Oh, My Dearest Daddy), Lauretta pleads with her father to help. He schemes to keep the outside world from knowing of the relative's death so Schicchi himself can pose as the dying man and change the will. The idea backfires on the greedy family when Schicchi dictates the changed terms, leaving all the money to himself!

Symphony No. 9 "From the New World" Fourth Movement Theme
Antonín Dvorák (1841-1904)

On November 27, 1892 the Czech composer Antonín Dvorák wrote to a friend, *"The Americans expect great things of me. I am to show them the way into the Promised Land, the realm of a new, independent art, in short a national style of music ..."* Dvorák began a term as artistic director and professor of composition at the National Conservatory of Music in New York beginning in 1892. His *Symphony No. 9* became his first composition written on American soil and contained music in the spirit of the folklore of black and Amerindian peoples. Its pentatonic scales, flatted leading tones, drone accompaniments, rhythmic ostinatos, and strongly syncopated rhythms give it a distinctly American flavor.

Funeral March Of A Marionette
Charles Gounod (1818-1893)

The French composer Charles Gounod wrote music of tender, lyrical charm. Ravel pronounced Gounod the 'founder of melody' in France. Yet, words inspired his best compositions and allowed him to create strong musical character studies such as those in his opera, *Faust,* the most successful opera of the 19th century. Another of Gounod's famous works, *Ave Maria,* bases its accompaniment on J.S. Bach's *Prelude No. 1 in C Major.* The film director Alfred Hitchcock used *Funeral March of a Marionette* as the theme music for his 1950's-era, televised mystery series.

Pilgrims' Chorus from the opera TANNHÄUSER
Richard Wagner (1813-1883)

The German composer Richard Wagner changed the face of music. He founded and directed the famous music theatre at Bayreuth, Germany, where he showcased his multi-hour music dramas. This new type of opera, which featured an entirely new synthesis of words and music, drew the attention of musicians and listeners throughout the world, who flocked to Bayreuth as if it were a musical Mecca and Wagner its god. Wagner based *Tannhäuser* on a medieval German legend, adding his own imagination and bits of history to the musical mix. *Tannhäuser* is a passionate, quarrelsome knight-minstrel, who has sought refuge from the grief of the world in the arms of the goddess Venus. The opera's location shifts between the supernatural world of the Goddess and the earthly world, symbolized by a fervent band of Christian pilgrims headed for Rome whose processional chorus recurs throughout the opera. At the end of the opera, *Tannhäuser* breaks Venus' spell over him by invoking the name of the Virgin Mary.

Symphony No. 7
Second Movement Theme

Ludwig van Beethoven (1770 – 1827)
Germany/Austria
originally for orchestra
Arranged by Mona Rejino

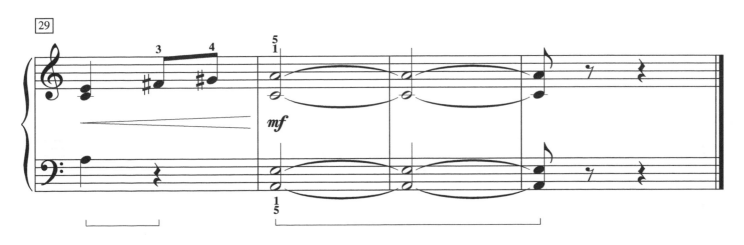

1812 Overture
Selected Themes

Pyotr Il'yich Tchaikovsky (1840 – 1893)
Russia
originally for orchestra
Arranged by Phillip Keveren

Allegro giusto (♩ = 110)

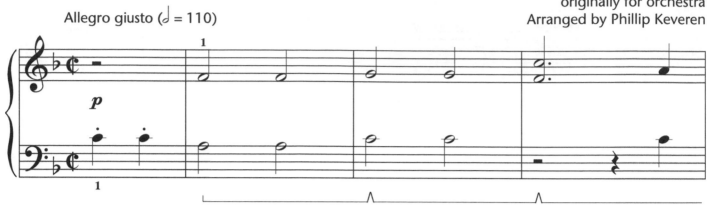

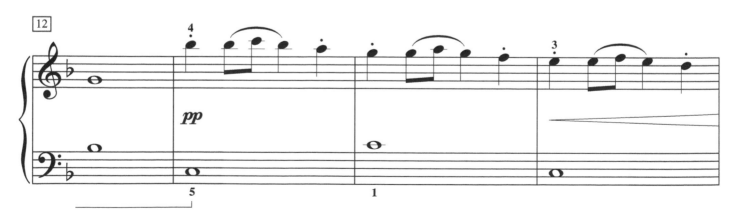

Allegro vivace (♩ = 126)

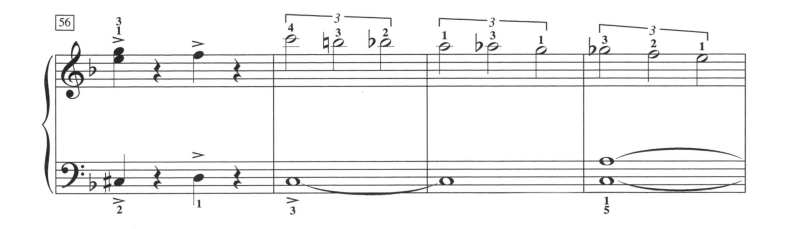

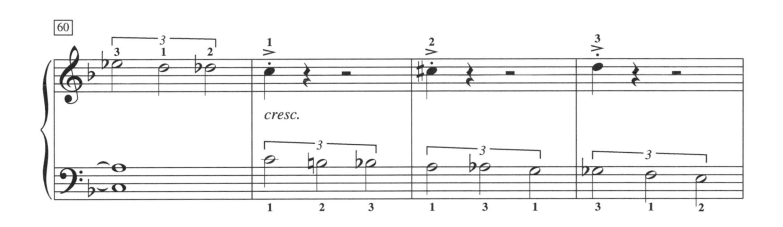

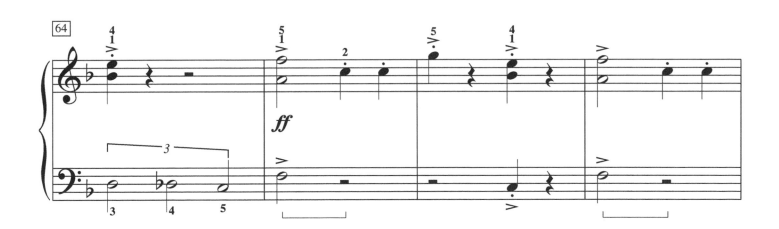

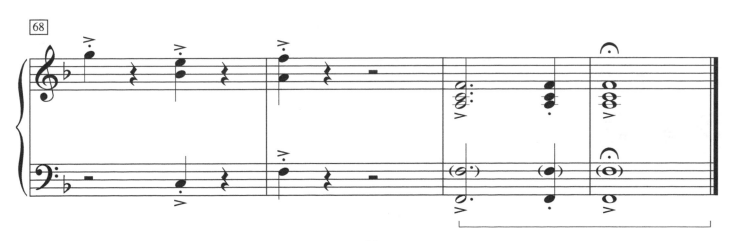

Symphony No. 6

"Pathetique"
First Movement Theme

Pyotr Il'yich Tchaikovsky (1840 – 1893)
Russia
originally for orchestra
Arranged by Fred Kern

Andante (♩ = 69)

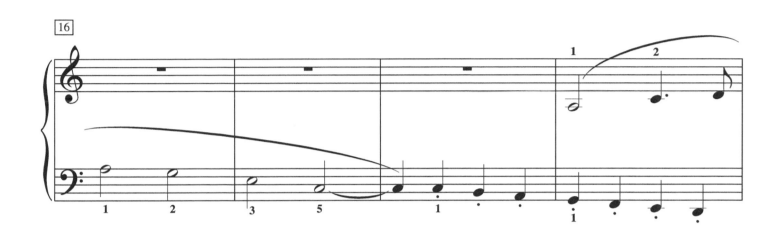

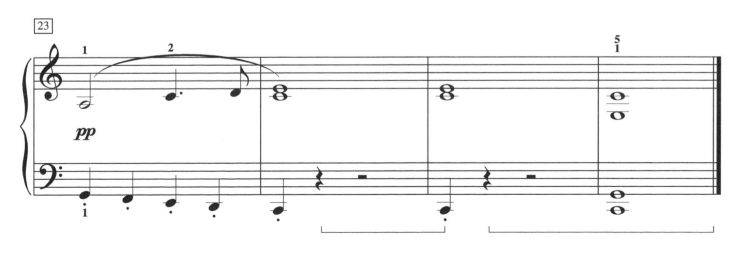

Carmen
Theme from the Overture

Georges Bizet (1838 – 1875)
France
originally for orchestra
Arranged by Mona Rejino

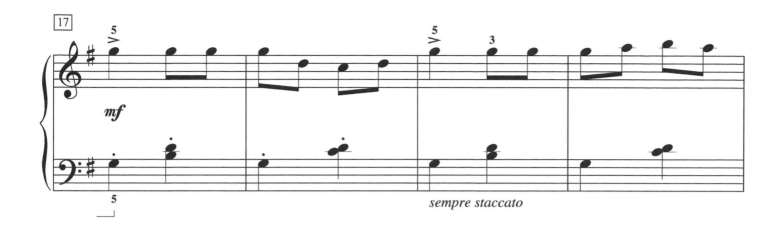

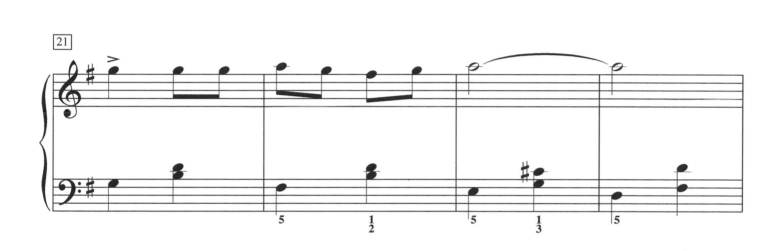

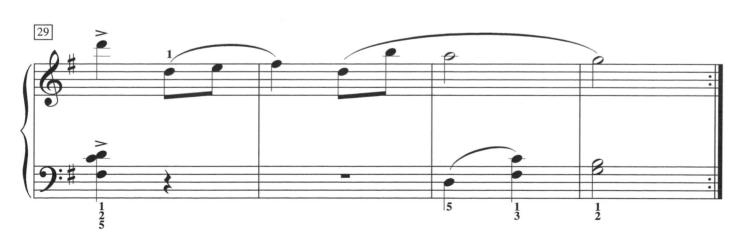

Ave Maria

Franz Schubert (1797 – 1828)
Austria
originally for voice and piano
Arranged by Fred Kern

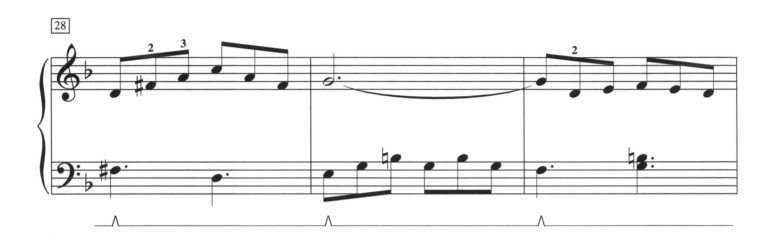

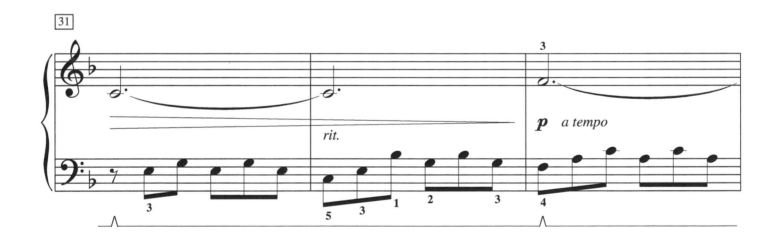

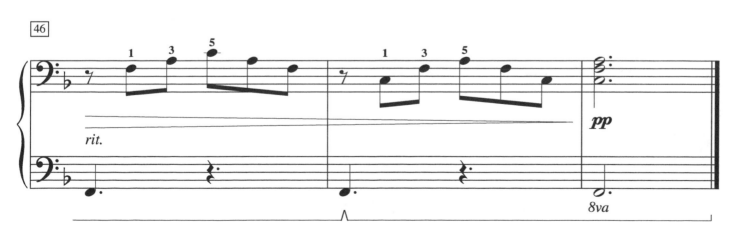

19

Rondeau

Jean-Joseph Mouret (1862 – 1738)
France
originally for chamber orchestra
Arranged by Fred Kern

Stately (♩ = 112)

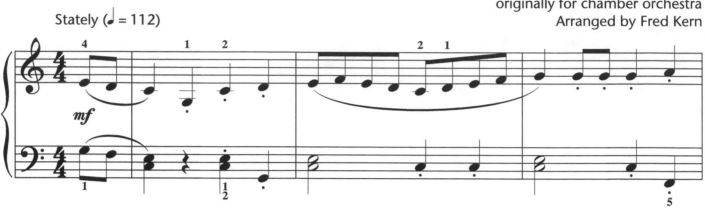

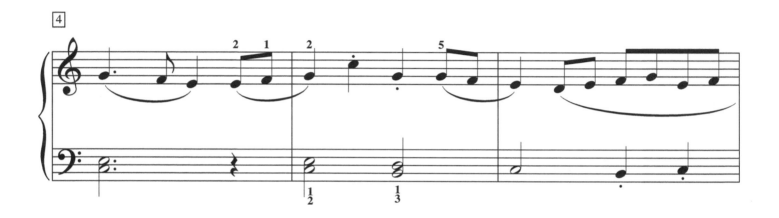

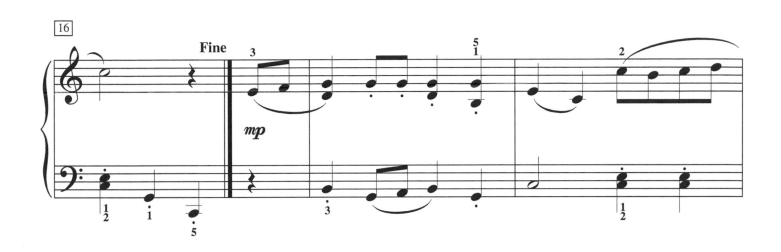

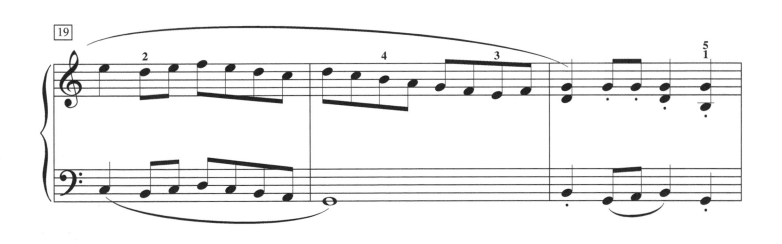

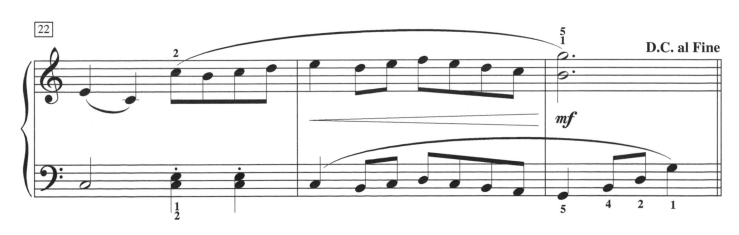

O mio babbino caro

from the opera GIANNI SCHICCHI

Giacomo Puccini (1858 – 1924)
Italy
originally for voice and orchestra
Arranged by Phillip Keveren

Andante (♩. = 44)

23

Symphony No. 9

"From The New World"
Fourth Movement Theme

Antonin Dvořák (1841 – 1904)
Czech Republic
originally for orchestra
Arranged by Phillip Keveren

Allegro con fuoco (♩ = 138)

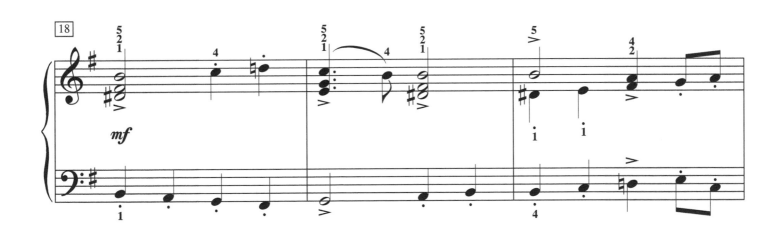

25

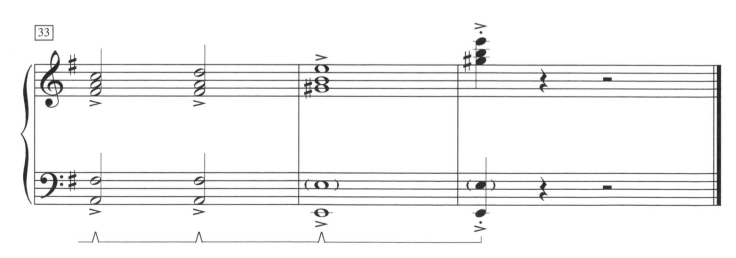

Funeral March Of A Marionette

Charles Gounod (1818 – 1893)
France
originally for piano solo; later orchestra
Arranged by Phillip Keveren

Pilgrims' Chorus

from the opera TANNHÄUSER

Richard Wagner (1813 – 1883)
Germany
originally for chorus and orchestra
Arranged by Mona Rejino

Andante maestoso (♩ = 76)

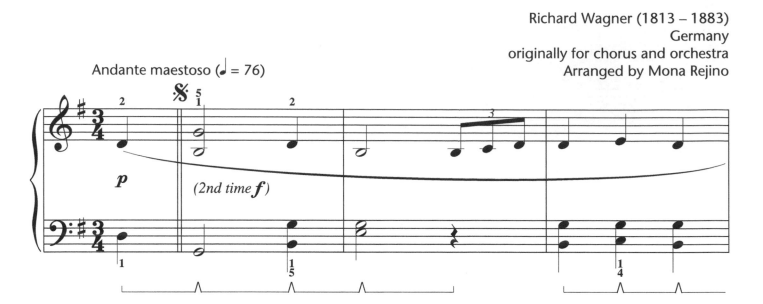

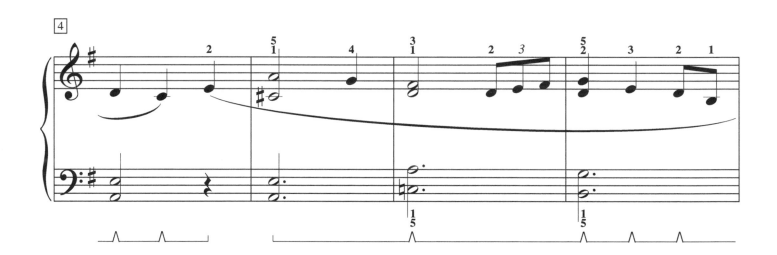

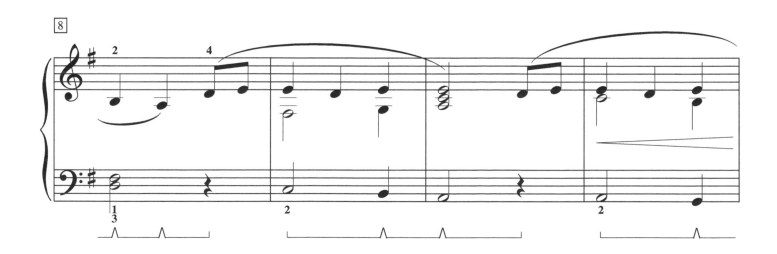

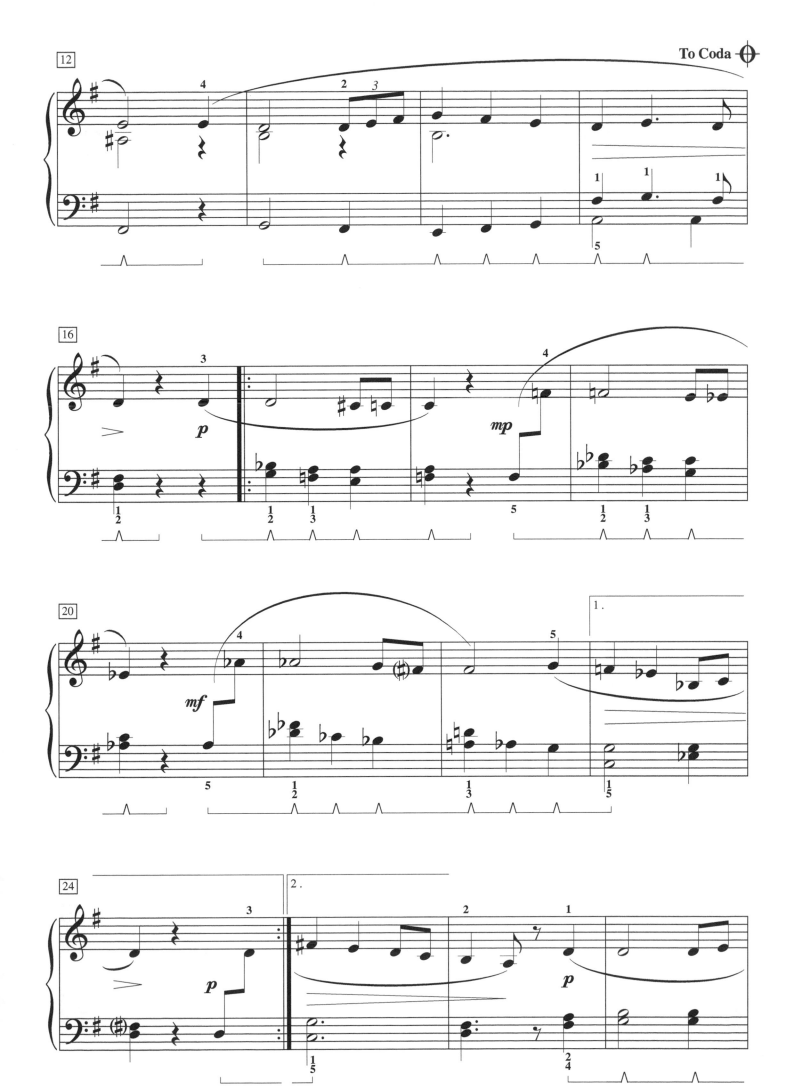

Music History Timeline

400 AD	600	800	1000	1200	1400

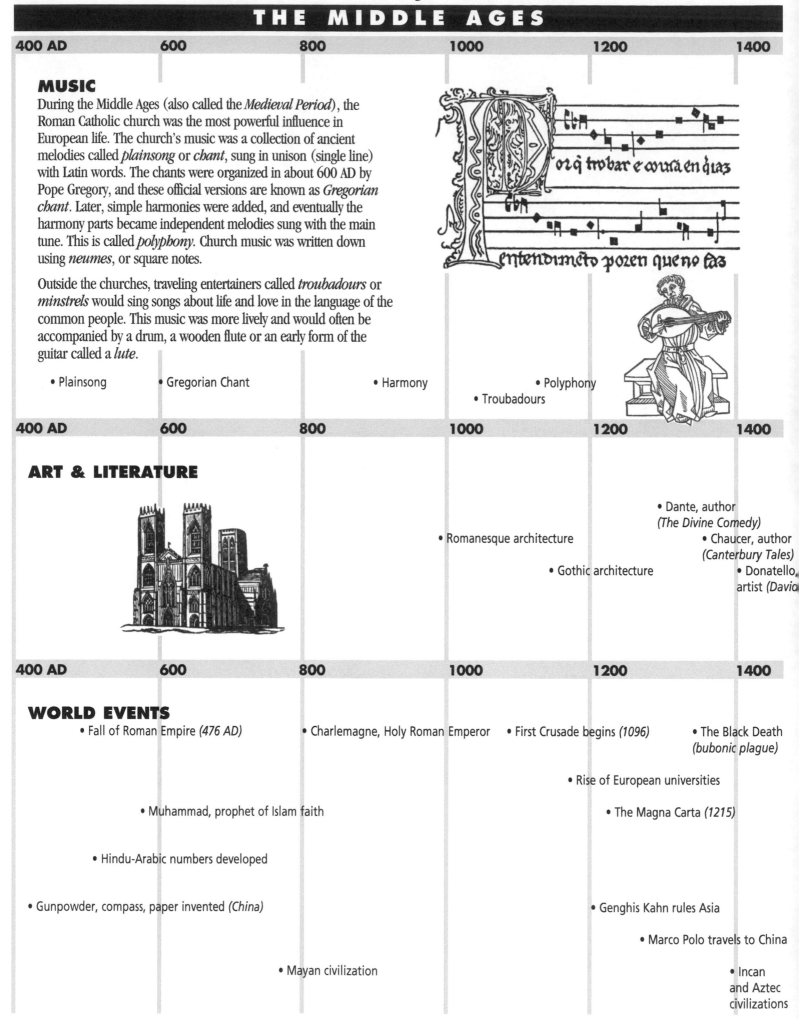

MUSIC

During the Middle Ages (also called the *Medieval Period*), the Roman Catholic church was the most powerful influence in European life. The church's music was a collection of ancient melodies called *plainsong* or *chant*, sung in unison (single line) with Latin words. The chants were organized in about 600 AD by Pope Gregory, and these official versions are known as *Gregorian chant*. Later, simple harmonies were added, and eventually the harmony parts became independent melodies sung with the main tune. This is called *polyphony*. Church music was written down using *neumes*, or square notes.

Outside the churches, traveling entertainers called *troubadours* or *minstrels* would sing songs about life and love in the language of the common people. This music was more lively and would often be accompanied by a drum, a wooden flute or an early form of the guitar called a *lute*.

- Plainsong
- Gregorian Chant
- Harmony
- Polyphony
- Troubadours

400 AD	600	800	1000	1200	1400

ART & LITERATURE

- Romanesque architecture
- Gothic architecture
- Dante, author *(The Divine Comedy)*
- Chaucer, author *(Canterbury Tales)*
- Donatello, artist *(David)*

400 AD	600	800	1000	1200	1400

WORLD EVENTS

- Fall of Roman Empire *(476 AD)*
- Charlemagne, Holy Roman Emperor
- First Crusade begins *(1096)*
- The Black Death *(bubonic plague)*
- Rise of European universities
- Muhammad, prophet of Islam faith
- The Magna Carta *(1215)*
- Hindu-Arabic numbers developed
- Gunpowder, compass, paper invented *(China)*
- Genghis Kahn rules Asia
- Marco Polo travels to China
- Mayan civilization
- Incan and Aztec civilizations

34

THE RENAISSANCE

1450	1500	1550	1600

MUSIC

The era from about 1450–1600 was called the *Renaissance* ("rebirth") because people wanted to recreate the artistic and scientific glories of ancient Greece and Rome. It was also a time of discovery. The new printing press brought music to the homes of the growing middle class. European society became more *secular*, or non-religious, and concerts were featured in the halls of the nobility. An entertaining form of secular songs was the *madrigal*, sung by 4 or 5 voices at many special occasions. Instrumental music became popular, as new string, brass and woodwind instruments were developed.

A form of church music was the *motet*, with 3 or 4 independent vocal parts. In the new Protestant churches, the entire congregation sang *chorales*: simple melodies in even rhythms like the hymns we hear today. Important Renaissance composers were Josquin des Pres, Palestrina, Gabrielli, Monteverdi, William Byrd and Thomas Tallis.

• Protestant church music

• First printed music • Madrigals

1450	1500	1550	1600

ART & LITERATURE

• Leonardo da Vinci, scientist/artist
(Mona Lisa, The Last Supper)

• Shakespeare, author
(Romeo and Juliet, Hamlet)

• Michelangelo, artist
(Sistine Chapel, David)

• Machiavelli,
author *(The Prince)*

1450	1500	1550	1600

WORLD EVENTS

• Gutenberg invents printing press *(1454)* • Martin Luther ignites Protestant Reformation *(1517)*

• Columbus travels to America *(1492)*

• Magellan circles globe *(1519)*

• Copernicus begins modern astronomy *(1543)*

• First European contact with Japan *(1549)*

THE BAROQUE ERA

1600	1650	1700	1750

MUSIC

Music and the arts (and even clothing) became fancier and more dramatic in the *Baroque* era (about 1600-1750). Like the fancy decorations of Baroque church architecture, melodies were often played with *grace notes*, or quick nearby tones added to decorate them. Rhythms became more complex with time signatures, bar lines and faster-moving melodic lines. Our now familiar major and minor scales formed the basis for harmony, and chords were standardized to what we often hear today.

The harpsichord became the most popular keyboard instrument, with players often *improvising* (making up) their parts using the composer's chords and bass line. Violin making reached new heights in Italy. Operas, ballets and small orchestras were beginning to take shape, as composers specified the exact instruments, tempos and dynamics to be performed.

• Jean Baptiste Lully, French *(1632-1687)*

• Henry Purcell, English *(1658-1695)*

• Francois Couperin, French *(1668-1733)*

• Georg Philipp Telemann, German *(1681-1767)*

• Jean-Philippe Rameau, French *(1683-1764)*

• George Frideric Handel, German *(1685-1759)*

• Domenico Scarlatti, Italian *(1685-1757)*

J.S. Bach

1600	1650	1700	1750

ART & LITERATURE

• Cervantes, author *(Don Quixote)*

• Rubens, artist *(Descent from the Cross)*

• Rembrandt, artist *(The Night Watch)*

• Taj Mahal built *(1634-1653)*

• Milton, author *(Paradise Lost)*

• Defoe, author *(Robinson Crusoe)*

• Kabuki theater in Japan

• Swift, author *(Gulliver's Travels)*

1600	1650	1700	1750

WORLD EVENTS

• Salem witchcraft trials *(1692)*

• Galileo identifies gravity *(1602)*

• Louis XIV builds Versailles Palace *(1661-1708)*

• First English colony in America *(Jamestown, 1607)*

• Quebec founded by Champlain *(1608)*

• First slaves to America *(1619)*

• Isaac Newton *(1642-1727)* formulates principals of physics and math

36

THE CLASSICAL ERA

1750	1775	1800	1820

MUSIC

The *Classical* era, from about 1750 to the early 1800's, was a time of great contrasts. While patriots fought for the rights of the common people in the American and French revolutions, composers were employed to entertain wealthy nobles and aristocrats. Music became simpler and more elegant, with melodies often flowing over accompaniment patterns in regular 4-bar phrases. Like the architecture of ancient *Classical* Greece, music was fit together in "building blocks" by balancing one phrase against another, or one entire section against another.

The piano replaced the harpsichord and became the most popular instrument for the *concerto* (solo) with orchestra accompaniment. The string quartet became the favorite form of *chamber* (small group) music, and orchestra concerts featured *symphonies* (longer compositions with 4 contrasting parts or *movements*). Toward the end of this era, Beethoven's changing musical style led the way toward the more emotional and personal expression of Romantic music.

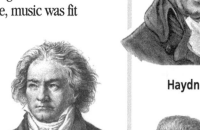
Haydn

Beethoven

Mozart

- Franz Haydn, Austrian (German) (1732-1809)
- Johann Christian Bach, German (1735-1782)
- Muzio Clementi, Italian (1752-1832)
- Wolfgang Amadeus Mozart, German (1756-1791)

- Ludwig van Beethoven, German (1770-1827)
- Antonio Diabelli, Italian (1781-1858)
- Friedrich Kuhlau, German (1786-1832)

1750	1775	1800	1820

ART & LITERATURE

- Samuel Johnson, author (Dictionary)

- Voltaire, author (Candide)

- Gainsborough, artist (The Blue Boy)

- Encyclopedia Britannica, first edition

- Wm. Wordsworth, author (Lyrical Ballads)

- Goethe, author (Faust)

- Goya, artist (Witch's Sabbath)

- Jane Austen, author (Pride and Prejudice)

1750	1775	1800	1820

WORLD EVENTS

- Ben Franklin discovers electricity (1751)

- American Revolution (1775-1783)

- French Revolution (1789-1794)

- Napoleon crowned Emperor of France (1804)

- Lewis and Clark explore northwest (1804)

- Metronome invented (1815)

- First steamship crosses Atlantic (1819)

THE ROMANTIC ERA

1820	1840	1860	1880	1900

MUSIC

The last compositions of Beethoven were among the first of the new *Romantic* era, lasting from the early 1800's to about 1900. No longer employed by churches or nobles, composers became free from Classical restraints and expressed their personal emotions through their music. Instead of simple titles like *Concerto* or *Symphony*, they would often add descriptive titles like *Witches' Dance* or *To The New World*. Orchestras became larger, including nearly all the standard instruments we now use. Composers began to write much more difficult and complex music, featuring more "colorful" instrument combinations and harmonies.

Nationalism was an important trend in this era. Composers used folk music and folk legends (especially in Russia, eastern Europe and Scandinavia) to identify their music with their native lands. Today's concert audiences still generally prefer the drama of Romantic music to any other kind.

Schumann

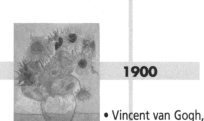

Brahms

- Franz Schubert, German *(1797-1828)*
- Felix Mendelssohn, German *(1809-1847)*
- Friedrich Burgmuller, German *(1806-1874)*
- Frederic Francois Chopin, Polish *(1810-1849)*
- Robert Schumann, German *(1810-1856)*
- Franz Liszt, Hungarian *(1811-1886)*
- Stephen Heller, German *(1813-1888)*
- Fritz Spindler, German *(1817-1905)*

- Cornelius Gurlitt, German *(1820-1901)*
- Cesar Auguste Franck, French *(1822-1890)*
- Johannes Brahms, German *(1833-1897)*
- Camille Saint-Saens, French *(1835-1921)*
- Modest Mussorgsky, Russian *(1839-1881)*
- Peter Ilyich Tchaikovsky, Russian *(1840-1893)*
- Edvard Grieg, Norwegian *(1844-1908)*

1820	1840	1860	1880	1900

ART & LITERATURE

- Charles Dickens, author *(The Pickwick Papers, David Copperfield)*

- Pierre Renoir, artist *(Luncheon of the Boating Party)*

- Harriet Beecher Stowe, author *(Uncle Tom's Cabin)*

- Lewis Carroll, author *(Alice In Wonderland)*

- Louisa May Alcott, author *(Little Women)*

- Jules Verne, author *(20,000 Leagues Under The Sea)*
- Claude Monet, artist *(Gare Saint-Lazare)*
- Mark Twain, author *(Tom Sawyer, Huckleberry Finn)*

- Vincent van Gogh, artist *(The Sunflowers)*
- Rudyard Kipling, author *(Jungle Book)*

1820	1840	1860	1880	1900

WORLD EVENTS

- First railroad *(1830)*
- Samuel Morse invents telegraph *(1837)*
- First photography *(1838)*

- American Civil War *(1861-1865)*

- Alexander Graham Bell invents telephone *(1876)*

- Edison invents phonograph, practical light bulb, movie projector *(1877-1888)*

THE 20th CENTURY

| 1900 | 1925 | 1950 | 1975 | 2000 |

- Edward MacDowell, American *(1861-1908)*
- Claude Debussy, French *(1862-1918)*
- Alexander Scriabin, Russian *(1872-1915)*
- Sergei Rachmaninoff, Russian *(1873-1943)*
- Arnold Schoenberg, German *(1874-1950)*
- Maurice Ravel, French *(1875-1937)*
- Bela Bartok, Hungarian *(1881-1945)*
- Heitor Villa-Lobos, Brazilian *(1881-1959)*
- Igor Stravinsky, Russian *(1882-1971)*
- Sergei Prokofieff, Russian *(1891-1952)*
- Paul Hindemith, German *(1895-1963)*
- George Gershwin, American *(1898-1937)*
- Aaron Copland, American *(1900-1990)*
- Aram Khachaturian, Russian *(1903-1978)*
- Dmitri Kabalevsky, Russian *(1904-1986)*
- Dmitri Shostakovich, Russian *(1906-1975)*
- Samuel Barber, American *(1910-1981)*
- Norman Dello Joio, American *(1913-   )*
- Vincent Persichetti, American *(1915-1987)*
- Philip Glass, American *(1937-   )*

MUSIC

The *20th century* was a diverse era of new ideas that "broke the rules" of traditional music. Styles of music moved in many different directions.

Impressionist composers Debussy and Ravel wrote music that seems more vague and blurred than the Romantics. New slightly-dissonant chords were used, and like Impressionist paintings, much of their music describes an impression of nature.

Composer Arnold Schoenberg devised a way to throw away all the old ideas of harmony by creating *12-tone* music. All 12 tones of the chromatic scale were used equally, with no single pitch forming a "key center."

Some of the music of Stravinsky and others was written in a *Neo-Classical* style (or "new" classical). This was a return to the Classical principals of balance and form, and to music that did *not* describe any scene or emotion.

Composers have experimented with many ideas: some music is based on the laws of chance, some is drawn on graph paper, some lets the performers decide when or what to play, and some is combined with electronic or other sounds.

Popular music like jazz, country, folk, and rock & roll has had a significant impact on 20th century life and has influenced great composers like Aaron Copland and Leonard Bernstein. And the new technology of computers and electronic instruments has had a major effect on the ways music is composed, performed and recorded.

| 1900 | 1925 | 1950 | 1975 | 2000 |

ART & LITERATURE

- Robert Frost, author *(Stopping by Woods on a Snowy Evening)*
- Pablo Picasso, artist *(Three Musicians)*
- J.R.R. Tolkien, author *(The Lord of the Rings)*
- F. Scott Fitzgerald, author *(The Great Gatsby)*
- Andy Warhol, artist *(Pop art)*
- Salvador Dali, artist *(Soft Watches)*
- Norman Mailer, author *(The Executioner's Song)*
- John Steinbeck, author *(The Grapes of Wrath)*
- Ernest Hemingway, author *(For Whom the Bell Tolls)*
- Andrew Wyeth, artist *(Christina's World)*
- George Orwell, author *(1984)*

| 1900 | 1925 | 1950 | 1975 | 2000 |

WORLD EVENTS

- First airplane flight *(1903)*
- Television invented *(1927)*
- Berlin Wall built *(1961)*
- Destruction of Berlin Wall *(1989)*
- World War I *(1914-1918)*
- World War II *(1939–1945)*
- John F. Kennedy assassinated *(1963)*
- First radio program *(1920)*
- Civil rights march in Alabama *(1965)*
- First satellite launched *(1957)*
- Man walks on the moon *(1969)*
- Vietnam War ends *(1975)*
- Personal computers *(1975)*

JOURNEY THROUGH THE
CLASSICS

COMPILED AND EDITED BY JENNIFER LINN

Journey Through the Classics is a four-volume piano repertoire series designed to lead students seamlessly from the easiest classics to the intermediate masterworks. The graded pieces are presented in a progressive order and feature a variety of classical favorites essential to any piano student's educational foundation. The authentic repertoire is ideal for auditions and recitals and each book includes a handy reference chart with the key, composer, stylistic period, and challenge elements listed for each piece. Quality and value make this series a perfect classical companion for any method.

BOOK 1 ELEMENTARY
00296870 Book Only............................$6.99
00142808 Book/Online Audio........$8.99

BOOK 2 LATE ELEMENTARY
00296871 Book Only............................$6.99
00142809 Book/Online Audio........$8.99

BOOK 3 EARLY INTERMEDIATE
00296872 Book Only............................$6.99
00142810 Book/Online Audio........$8.99

www.halleonard.com

BOOK 4 INTERMEDIATE
00296873 Book Only..........................$7.99
00142811 Book/Online Audio........$9.99

JOURNEY THROUGH
THE CLASSICS COMPLETE
(all 4 levels included in one book)
00110217 Book Only........................$17.99
00123124 Book/Online Audio.....$24.99

Prices, contents, and availability subject to change without notice.